LIFE IN THE SPECIAL FORCES

LIFE AS A
NAVY SEAL

by Tammy Gagne

BrightPoint Press

San Diego, CA

© 2024 BrightPoint Press
an imprint of ReferencePoint Press, Inc.
Printed in the United States

For more information, contact:
BrightPoint Press
PO Box 27779
San Diego, CA 92198
www.BrightPointPress.com

ALL RIGHTS RESERVED.

No part of this work covered by the copyright hereon may be reproduced or used in any form or by any means—graphic, electronic, or mechanical, including photocopying, recording, taping, web distribution, or information storage retrieval systems—without the written permission of the publisher.

LIBRARY OF CONGRESS CATALOGING-IN-PUBLICATION DATA

Names: Gagne, Tammy, author.
Title: Life as a Navy SEAL / by Tammy Gagne.
Description: San Diego, CA: BrightPoint, [2024] | Series: Life in the special forces | Includes bibliographical references and index. | Audience: Grades 7–9
Identifiers: LCCN 2023036083 (print) | LCCN 2023036084 (eBook) | ISBN 9781678207427 (hardcover) | ISBN 9781678207434 (eBook)
Subjects: LCSH: United States. Navy. SEALs--Juvenile literature. | United States. Navy. SEALs--Military life--Juvenile literature. | United States. Navy--Commando troops--Juvenile literature.
Classification: LCC VG87 .G34 2024 (print) | LCC VG87 (eBook) | DDC 359.9/84--dc23/eng/20230803
LC record available at https://lccn.loc.gov/2023036083
LC eBook record available at https://lccn.loc.gov/2023036084

CONTENTS

AT A GLANCE	4
INTRODUCTION MISSION ACCOMPLISHED	6
CHAPTER ONE BECOMING A NAVY SEAL	12
CHAPTER TWO NAVY SEAL EQUIPMENT	24
CHAPTER THREE THE WORK OF NAVY SEALs	36
CHAPTER FOUR NAVY SEAL MISSIONS	46
Glossary	58
Source Notes	59
For Further Research	60
Index	62
Image Credits	63
About the Author	64

AT A GLANCE

- US Navy SEALs are special forces troops in the US military. Their name stands for "sea, air, and land."

- The standards for becoming a SEAL are extremely high. Only about one-quarter of people who go through the long and demanding training graduate.

- Navy SEALs who perform underwater missions often travel in SEAL delivery vehicles (SDVs). These mini submarines can hold up to six people.

- Navy SEALs often use weapons such as M4 carbines and Mk-24 handguns.

- SEALs who want to specialize as snipers must graduate from the Navy SEAL Sniper Course. The program lasts 3 months.

- SEAL specialties include communications and demolitions.

- In 2011, Navy SEALs performed one of the most famous special forces missions in history. They found and killed terrorist Osama bin Laden.

- Not all Navy SEAL missions involve combat. Sometimes SEALs rescue people in danger.

INTRODUCTION

MISSION ACCOMPLISHED

Alec and Henry had been treading water for hours. They could barely feel their arms and legs. But they kept moving to stay afloat. US Navy SEALs never quit.

Henry oversaw communications. He held his waterproof radio to his ear and nodded to Alec. Four of their teammates had just rescued a **hostage**. It was an American journalist. Henry listened to local radio chatter. Word about the rescue hadn't spread yet.

Two SEAL snipers lay on a nearby roof. They were ready to shoot anyone who threatened the journalist or the SEALs. The rescuers sped toward the rest of the team in a pickup truck. Rounding a corner in the distance, the enemy forces pursued them.

There are many different roles in the SEALs, including snipers.

SEALs often use helicopters to travel to and from their missions.

Alec made sure everyone crossed a nearby bridge. He then prepared to set off C4 explosives. Alec was the team's **demolitions** expert. He had placed the powerful explosives earlier. When he set them off, they would blow the bridge to pieces.

This would buy the group enough time to reach a US Navy helicopter. Its pilot was ready to fly the Americans to the nearest US military base. The SEALs and the journalists disappeared into the woods. A thunderous boom echoed over the water behind them. The hostage rescue mission was a success.

WHO ARE THE NAVY SEALs?

The Navy SEALs are a special operations force that performs dangerous missions.

Sometimes SEALs capture or kill terrorists. Other times they rescue friendly targets. These may include **civilians** or fellow troops. Whatever the mission is, SEALs must give their all to make it a success.

The name *SEAL* is a combination of the settings where these soldiers work. SEALs operate in the sea, in the air, and on land. Some missions involve all three. SEAL training is not easy. Those who complete it become members of one of the most elite special forces in the world.

SEALs may be best known for their work in the water, but they go on missions in all kinds of environments.

1
BECOMING A NAVY SEAL

The first step to becoming a Navy SEAL is joining the US Navy. Applicants must take the Armed Services Vocational Aptitude Battery (ASVAB). This series of tests is designed to identify strengths and weaknesses in a variety of subjects. The Navy requires a score of at least 35 out of 99 on part of the ASVAB called the Armed Forces Qualification Test (AFQT).

Most future SEALs score at least 78 on this part of the exam.

Navy SEALs must be between 17 and 28 years old at the start of training. They need a high school degree or general equivalency

People joining the military can use apps to practice for the ASVAB tests.

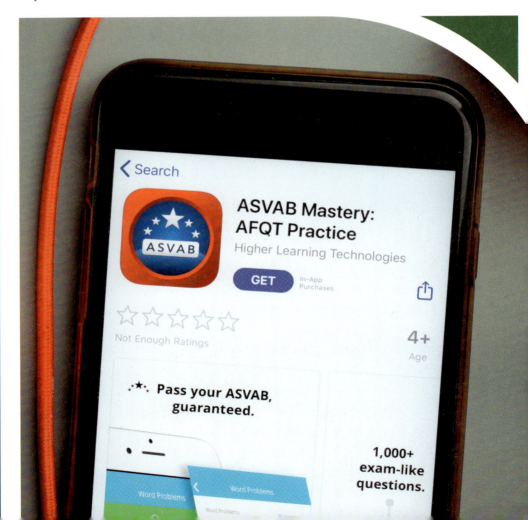

diploma (GED). Both men and women can apply.

Navy SEALS must be in excellent physical condition. The Navy's general physical screening test (PST) is tough. People must complete a 500-yard (457-m) swim in less than 12.5 minutes. They must also finish a 1.5-mile (2.4-km) run in less than 9.5 minutes. SEAL training has even higher standards. Applicants must finish those two exercises in less than 9 minutes each.

THE TRAITS OF NAVY SEALs

Navy SEALs must be physically and mentally strong. They conduct some of the most dangerous operations in the military. They must remain calm under stress.

Physical fitness is key for Navy SEALs.

SEAL training is intense and challenging.

These soldiers must be able to focus on the task in front of them.

Pushing oneself physically can be mentally demanding. When pushed to their limits, people may want to quit. But **perseverance** can mean the difference between success and failure for SEALs. Sean Haggerty often doubted himself when he was training as a SEAL. But he says, "Don't confuse doubting yourself with accepting failure. The best thing I did was to decide that I was going to go the absolute extreme, even if I doubted myself."[1]

SEALs perform some tasks alone. But they accomplish their missions by working with other SEALs. Former SEAL Diego Ugalde explained that working as part of a team made him better. He said,

"The best of me is no comparison to what could be created through teams. Let go of your ego and fear of losing control and see what genius lies within your team. Mistakes are nearly irrelevant. What can be learned from those mistakes is as useful as any 'success.'"[2]

TRAINING TO BECOME A NAVY SEAL

The first part of Navy SEAL training takes place in Coronado, California. It is called Basic Underwater Demolition/SEAL (BUD/S) school. BUD/S is made up of three phases. It is one of the most demanding training programs among all US special forces.

The first phase lasts 8 weeks. It includes 4-mile (6.4-km) beach runs, 2-mile (3.2-km) swims, and obstacle courses that are swum

SEAL candidates in the first phase work together to lift a 600-pound (272-kg) log.

Practicing parachuting with a full load of gear prepares SEALs for future missions.

with fins. The second phase of BUD/S takes another 8 weeks. It focuses on diving skills. SEALs must use math to plan safe dives. By the end of this phase, candidates complete a 6-mile (9.7-km) ocean swim. The third phase focuses on land warfare. It is 9 weeks long. This part includes intense training in weapons, demolition, and **rappelling**.

Former SEAL Brad McLeod thinks mental strength helps people complete this challenging training. He shares, "It has been said that the training is 80 percent mental and 20 percent physical. I firmly believe that."[3] When McLeod went through BUD/S, he saw many physically fit applicants give up due to mental stress.

People who complete BUD/S move on to Parachute Jump School at Fort Benning,

Georgia. They spend 3 weeks learning to jump from airplanes while carrying combat equipment. Jumps take place at a minimum of 9,500 feet (2,900 m) in the air. Candidates return to Coronado for Seal Qualification Training (SQT). This is the longest training phase yet. It lasts for 26 weeks and teaches people how to perform SEAL missions. They learn survival skills, combat skills, and other parts of warfare.

HOW MANY SAILORS RECEIVE THE TRIDENT?

Only a small number of people who want to become a US Navy SEAL succeed. Just 6 percent of those who apply are accepted into the training program. Of those who enter training, only about 26 percent graduate.

Those who remain will become US Navy SEALs. All SEALs are given a gold **trident** pin as a symbol of this accomplishment. But their training is still far from over. New SEALs must spend the next 18 months in advanced training. During this time, SEALs continue practicing the skills they have learned. This further prepares them for real missions.

2
NAVY SEAL EQUIPMENT

Navy SEALs need a variety of equipment to perform their missions. This includes vehicles. Many missions depend on sneaking into an area without being noticed by the enemy.

SEAL delivery vehicles (SDVs) are mini submarines. They transport SEALs to and from underwater missions. The Mark 11 SDV can carry up to six SEALs at one time.

It is 23 feet (7 m) long. The vessel can dive 165 feet (50 m) below the ocean's surface.

The Mark 11 fills with water when in use. SEALs must use oxygen tanks to breathe. *Popular Mechanics* writer Kyle Mizokami

SDVs give SEALs a way to sneak into enemy territory underwater.

pointed out that spending hours in an SDV is uncomfortable. He wrote, "The ride is best compared to a small car or airplane, with no room to stand, no room to lie down, and no bathroom."[4]

SEALs often travel over water in a combat rubber raiding craft (CRRC). This inflatable boat can carry ten passengers. SEALS can parachute with a CRRC from a plane. They can also carry it on an SDV. SEALs can use a small motor to move fast in a CRRC. They may paddle it if they need to be quieter.

The rigid hull inflatable boat (RHIB) isn't as compact as the CRRC. But the RHIB is often a smarter choice when speed is needed. It has two engines. Each is about eight times more powerful than the CRRC's single engine. This makes the RHIB

A RHIB gives SEALs both speed and firepower.

much faster. It can also operate in rough sea waves and high winds. This makes it a good boat for dangerous weather.

NAVY SEAL WEAPONS

Navy SEALs carry handguns on nearly all their missions. Most other military members use the Beretta M9 pistol. But SEALs operate in salt water, mud, and sandy areas. They need a handgun that will stand up to these damaging elements. SEALs carry the SIG Sauer P226 for this reason. Also called the Mk-25, this gun is made with stainless steel to resist **corrosion**. It has a 4.4-inch (11.2-cm) barrel and weighs less than 2 pounds (0.9 kg). It is both shorter and lighter than the M9. The gun's small size makes it easier to handle.

SEALs also carry rifles. The most common is the M4A1 carbine. This weapon was designed specifically for US special forces. It is based on the M16A2, which

The M4A1 carbine is widely used in the US military.

much of the US military uses. But it is nearly 10 inches (25 cm) shorter. This makes it easier to aim and fire at close range. The M4A1 can be equipped with sights, lasers, and flashlights. This allows SEALs to adapt the rifle to each mission.

SEALs sometimes need more powerful weapons. The M4A1 can be fitted with an M203 grenade launcher. It can hit targets from 1,150 feet (350 m) away. But it

SNIPER RIFLES

US Navy SEAL snipers shoot targets at long range. They use a wide variety of rifles. Some of the most powerful are the Mk-15 and M82. Each of these weapons shoots a .50 caliber round. They can be used against not only enemy soldiers but also lightly armored vehicles.

adds 3.5 pounds (1.6 kg) to the weight of the rifle. Many SEALs prefer to use the M320 grenade launcher instead. It is a stand-alone weapon. However, combining a rifle and grenade launcher can be helpful when space is limited.

Another powerful weapon SEALs use is the M2 machine gun. It is also one of the heaviest. It weighs more than 83 pounds (38 kg). Its .50 caliber rounds can hit a target from more than 1.1 miles (1.8 km) away. SEALs can mount the M2 on a **tripod** to fire it from the ground. They can also attach it to a land vehicle, boat, or aircraft. The M2 can penetrate armor, vehicles, or even concrete walls. This machine gun is one of the oldest weapons used by the US military. It was

High-tech gear helps SEALs breathe and move underwater.

designed in the 1920s. It remains a trusted weapon today.

OTHER IMPORTANT SEAL TOOLS

The tools SEALs need vary by the mission. Navy SEALs use diving equipment similar to that used by civilian divers. This includes air tanks, dive fins, and masks. But SEALs usually wear a full face mask. It helps them see better and protects them from pollution in dirty water.

SEALs use parachutes when jumping from planes. For high-altitude jumps, they may need to carry breathing oxygen. They may also use devices that automatically open the parachute at a set height. This can save their lives if they black out during the jump.

Night-vision gear gives SEALs an advantage over enemies in dark environments.

SEALs carry communications and navigation gear. These may include radios and GPS devices. They also use advanced night-vision goggles and underwater drones. Compact cameras help them gather important intelligence. But SEALs do not rely too much on their equipment. Former SEAL Jocko Willink says the brain is the most important tool that a SEAL has.

3
THE WORK OF NAVY SEALs

New recruits and established sailors can become Navy SEALs. Sailors with ranks between E-1 and E-9 are called enlisted service members. Each level comes with its own amount of responsibility and pay. Enlisted members can be promoted by performing well. A sailor graduates from BUD/S with at least the rank of E-4, or petty officer third class.

Sailors who continue their education can become officers. People with a bachelor's degree can also join the Navy as officers. Officer ranks range from O-1 to O-10. These sailors also move up in rank by earning promotions. The biggest differences between enlisted Navy SEALs and officers

Graduates of SEAL training programs earn a trident pin.

are leadership roles and pay. Each step up in rank comes with more responsibility. It also offers more base pay. But the Navy needs ten times more enlisted SEALs than officers. For this reason, many people with college degrees choose to begin SEAL training as enlisted service members.

SEAL trainers expect officers in SEAL training to demonstrate leadership skills. Officers' extra military experience helps them make it through the training. In 2022, officers training to become SEALs had a training success rate of 89 percent.

APPLYING THEIR SKILLS

All Navy SEALs are trained to handle guns, jump from planes, and dive deep into the ocean. But some SEALs train

SEAL snipers learn to hide from enemy view while completing their missions.

further for a special role on a team. SEALs with exceptional firearm skills may attend the Navy SEAL Sniper Course. It lasts 3 months. Each week includes 100 hours of training with no days off.

Students learn how to move quietly and hide in different environments. Students also shoot at targets from at least 1,094 yards (1,000 m) away. Some of these targets stay still while others move or pop up. The students also practice shooting in windy conditions. Former Navy SEAL sniper Brandon Webb says the course takes perseverance. He explains, "To this day it was one of the most stressful events

OPERATING IN THE COLD

Movies about Navy SEALs often show them on missions in hot deserts or steamy jungles. But real SEALs must work in a variety of climates. They may be sent to cold woodland areas or even arctic regions.

of my life even when compared to my combat tours."[5]

SEALS can also specialize in communications, demolitions, and even foreign languages. The needs of each mission are different. One assignment may take a SEAL to capture a terrorist. Another might require the team to rescue a soldier. Each SEAL's responsibilities will also differ somewhat from one mission to the next. If things don't go as expected, the team may even need to change these tasks in the middle of a mission.

MOVING FORWARD

SEALs can retire from the Navy after 20 years of service. But many prefer to stay 30. This significantly increases their

SEAL instructors train the next generation of special forces troops.

retirement pay. If SEALs choose to stay in the Navy, it doesn't mean they have to keep going on missions. After working on a team for a while, some SEALs become trainers. Serving as an instructor at BUD/S is just one example of how SEALs can use their knowledge and skills. Successful Navy SEAL training requires people who know what it takes to do this job.

All SEALs begin their careers performing missions. They may keep working in the field for the rest of their Navy careers. But after two or more operations, most enlisted SEALs have chosen a specialty. Officers often move to higher-ranking positions after working in the field for a while. These jobs may mean working in an office instead. But officers can still play important roles in missions. These SEALs take on the responsibility of planning the operations. They use their education and experience to help make sure each mission is a success.

SEALs can leave the military at the end of an enlistment period. This is the amount of time that service members agree to remain in the military. Many SEALs use their special forces experience to pursue other careers after leaving the military. Some go into private security. Other SEALs have had second careers as business owners, pilots, and even writers. Jack Carr writes best-selling novels about Navy SEALs.

Michael Crooke spent 4 years as a SEAL. He then earned his master's degree in business. He started working for the outdoor clothing company Patagonia. He became its chief executive officer in 1999. Today, Crooke is a college professor.

NASA astronaut Jonny Kim is a former Navy SEAL.

He credits the teamwork he learned as a SEAL to his success. He says, "All of the lessons I learned in the teams have helped me all along the way."[6]

ated lifeboat. But they took Phillips with them as a hostage.

4
NAVY SEAL MISSIONS

In 2009, pirates hijacked the *Maersk Alabama* in the Indian Ocean. Four men snuck onto the US cargo ship in the Indian Ocean. They used rifles to threaten Captain Richard Phillips and take control of the ship. When Phillips and his crew fought back, the pirates escaped in a motorized lifeboat. But they took Phillips with them as a hostage.

They threatened to kill him unless the United States paid them $2 million.

The White House sent SEAL Team Six. The SEALs traveled 8,000 miles (12,875 km) for the mission. No one knows for sure how the team got to the area.

An image from a military drone shows the Maersk Alabama lifeboat as Navy SEALs planned the rescue mission.

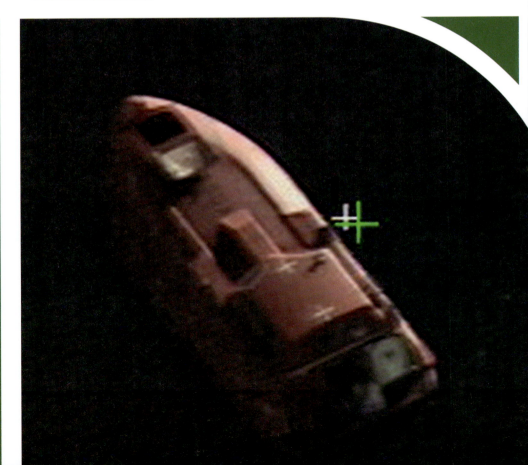

But retired Rear Admiral Terry McKnight shared his thoughts. He wrote, "SEALs are understandably concerned about stealth. That tells me that the operation was planned so they would parachute into the ocean under the cover of darkness."[7]

One pirate had been injured on the *Maersk Alabama*. He surrendered in exchange for medical help. But the others refused to give up. When Phillips tried to escape, one of the remaining pirates fired his weapon. The round went into the water. The SEALs knew it was time to act. SEAL snipers killed all three remaining pirates.

FINDING OSAMA BIN LADEN

One of the most famous Navy SEAL missions took place in Abbottabad,

Pakistan. The US military had been searching for Osama bin Laden since 2001. He was the mastermind behind the September 11 attacks on the United States. In these attacks, terrorists hijacked airliners and flew them into buildings. Nearly 3,000 people were killed.

As the leader of al Qaeda, bin Laden continued to plan terror attacks in hiding.

THE MEDAL OF HONOR

Lieutenant Michael Murphy's SEAL team became trapped by enemies in the mountains of Afghanistan in 2003. He was shot after stepping into the open to call for help on his satellite phone. Still, he completed the call to save his teammates. He died from his wounds. Following his heroic death, Murphy was awarded the Medal of Honor. This is the top US military honor. Only six other SEALs have received it.

President Barack Obama, second from left, watched with other officials as the SEALs carried out the raid in Pakistan.

But the US military never stopped searching for him. On May 2, 2011, two dozen Navy SEALs raided the compound in Abbottabad where bin Laden hid. The mission was called Neptune Spear. The SEALs arrived in stealth helicopters whose existence had previously been secret. Within minutes, they found and killed bin Laden.

The following day, President Barack Obama gave a speech to the nation. In it, he said, "A small team of Americans carried out the operation with extraordinary courage and capability." He pointed out that that no Americans were harmed. Later in the address, he said, "The death of bin Laden marks the most significant achievement to date in our nation's effort to defeat al Qaeda."[8]

LESSER-KNOWN MISSIONS

Civilians do not hear about most US Navy SEAL missions. Often, they involve sensitive information. Sharing it with the public could put many lives in danger. But not all missions involve well-known targets. Some Navy SEAL operations save everyday people in danger. This was the case in 2020 when the Navy SEALs rescued Philip Walton in Nigeria.

Walton lived with his family in Massalata, Niger. He made his living as a farmer close to the border with Nigeria. A criminal gang from that country entered his backyard on October 26, 2020. They asked Walton for money, and he gave them $40. But they kidnapped him in hopes of trading the American for more money.

Navy SEALs worked with the governments of Niger and Nigeria on this mission. The United States learned where the gang was holding Walton in northern Nigeria. News reports of the operation included few details. But they confirmed

US troops have trained in Nigeria in cooperation with the Nigerian government.

that the SEALs rescued Walton unharmed on October 31.

Another lesser-known mission took place in April 2023. As the nation of Sudan fought a violent civil war, Navy SEALs headed to the region. Their mission was to **evacuate** the US embassy in the country. It was no longer safe for Americans to stay there.

SEAL Team Six flew in two MH-47 Chinook helicopters. They traveled from the nation of Djibouti to Khartoum, Sudan. They left before dawn so they wouldn't be seen. This strategy worked. The aircraft arrived without being fired upon.

The SEAL team led about 100 people to six airplanes that took them out of the country. Most of these people were Americans. They included US Marines who provided security for the embassy. But the

Large Chinook helicopters can carry many troops into action at once.

SEAL MISSION LOCATIONS

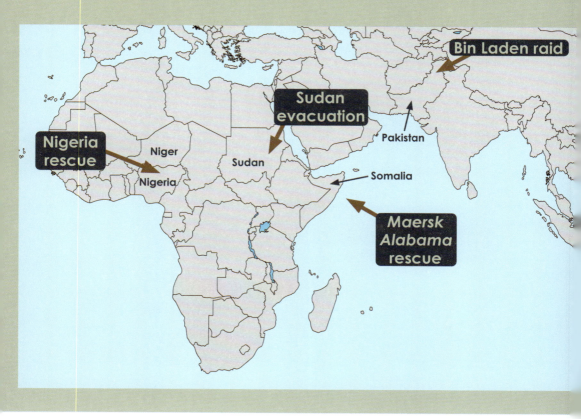

US Navy SEALs perform their missions in many countries. For this reason, SEALs sometimes learn a foreign language.

group also included other people whose lives were endangered. The White House described the mission as fast and clean. The rescue was a success.

Being a Navy SEAL is one of the most difficult jobs in the US military. The missions of these special force members are dangerous. But SEALs' courage, strength, and sacrifice are among the many reasons they are one of the most respected special forces in the world today.

GLOSSARY

civilians

people who are not members of the military

corrosion

wearing away gradually through a chemical reaction

demolitions

destructions by means of explosives

evacuate

to move people from danger to a safer place

hostage

a person held against their will by another person, often to exchange for something

perseverance

dedicated effort despite difficulties

rappelling

descending by sliding down a rope that is placed under one's leg

trident

a three-pronged spear

tripod

a three-legged stand that supports equipment such as a gun

SOURCE NOTES

CHAPTER ONE: BECOMING A NAVY SEAL

1. Quoted in Jeff Haden, "The Navy SEAL Approach to Persistence, Resilience, and Success," *US Veterans Magazine*, n.d. https://usveteransmagazine.com.

2. Quoted in Adam Mendler, "Interview with Former Navy SEAL Diego Ugalde," *Adam Mendler*, n.d. www.adammendler.com.

3. Quoted in Zach Even, "Navy SEAL Interview, Part II with Brad McLeod," *Zach Even*, n.d., https://zacheven-esh.com.

CHAPTER TWO: NAVY SEAL EQUIPMENT

4. Kyle Mizokami, "This Mini-Sub Is Like a Commuter Bus for Navy SEAL Commandos," *Popular Mechanics*, January 22, 2020. www.popularmechanics.com.

CHAPTER THREE: THE WORK OF NAVY SEALS

5. Brandon Webb, "The Navy SEAL Elite Sniper Program," *SOFREP*, August 21, 2021. https://sofrep.com.

6. Quoted in Nick Coffman, "How the Navy SEALs Prepare for a Successful Life After the Teams," *SOFREP*, March 14, 2016. https://sofrep.com.

CHAPTER FOUR: NAVY SEAL MISSIONS

7. Quoted in David Axe, "Inside a Navy SEAL Rescue," *Wired*, October 17, 2012. www.wired.com.

8. Quoted in "Osama bin Laden Dead," *White House*, May 2, 2011. https://obamawhitehouse.archives.gov.

FOR FURTHER RESEARCH

BOOKS

Tammy Gagne, *The Armed Forces Encyclopedia*. Minneapolis, MN: Abdo, 2024.

Cynthia Kennedy Henzel, *Life as a Green Beret*. San Diego, CA: BrightPoint Press, 2024.

Howard Phillips, *Inside the Navy SEALs*. New York: PowerKids Press, 2022.

INTERNET SOURCES

"Medal of Honor Monday: Navy Lt. Michael P. Murphy," *US Department of Defense*, June 27, 2022. www.defense.gov.

"Navy SEALs: Background and Brief History," *Military.com*, n.d. www.military.com.

"'Quiet Professionals' Dazzle in Training," *US Department of Defense*, February 9, 2023. www.defense.gov.

WEBSITES

Navy SEAL Museum
www.navysealmuseum.org/naval-special-warfare

The Navy SEAL Museum honors Navy SEALS by preserving the history and heritage of this special force. Its website includes a virtual memorial wall that honors SEALs lost in combat since World War II.

Official Naval Special Warfare Website
www.sealswcc.com/navy-seal-swcc-who-we-are-main.html

The Official Naval Special Warfare website offers civilians a look at the work of Navy SEALs. It includes photos, videos, and podcasts about many aspects of SEAL life.

US Navy Seals
www.navy.com/seals

The US Navy SEALS website offers detailed information about the path to becoming a Navy SEAL. People interested in this military career can learn more about the requirements and responsibilities of SEALs here.

INDEX

bin Laden, Osama, 48–51, 56
boats, 26–27, 31

Coronado, California, 18, 22
Crooke, Michael, 44–45

diving, 21, 33, 38

equipment, 33–35
explosives, 9

grenade launchers, 30–31

Haggerty, Sean, 17
handguns, 28
helicopters, 9, 50–51, 54
hostages, 6, 9, 46

joining the military, 12–13

machine guns, 31–33
Maersk Alabama rescue, 46–48
McLeod, Brad, 21
Medal of Honor, 49
Murphy, Michael, 49

Nigeria, 52, 56
night vision, 35

Obama, Barack, 51

Pakistan, 48–51, 56
parachuting, 21–22, 26, 33, 48
Phillips, Richard, 46, 48
physical fitness, 14

ranks, 36–38
rifles, 28–31
roles, 38–41

SEAL delivery vehicle (SDV), 24–26
snipers, 7, 30, 39, 40, 48
Sudan, 54, 56

teamwork, 17–18, 41, 45, 49
terrorists, 10, 41, 49
training, 10, 13–23, 38–39, 43

Walton, Philip, 52–54
Webb, Brandon, 40
Willink, Jocko, 35

IMAGE CREDITS

Cover: © Chief Photographer's Mate Andrew McKaskle/US Navy
5: © Petty Officer 3rd Class Adam Henderson/US Navy/DVIDS
7: © Sgt. Hannah Hawkins/US Army/DVIDS
8: © Petty Officer 2nd Class Scott Raegen/US Navy/DVIDS
11: © DVIDS
13: © Postmodern Studio/Shutterstock Images
15: © Petty Officer 1st Class Leslie Long/US Navy/DVIDS
16: © Petty Officer 3rd Class Dylan Lavin/US Navy/DVIDS
19: © Petty Officer 2nd Class Shauntae Hinkle-Lymas/US Navy/DVIDS
20: © Petty Officer 1st Class Shannon Renfroe/US Navy/DVIDS
25: © US Navy/DVIDS
27: © Petty Officer 2nd Class Matt Daniels/US Navy/DVIDS
29: © Steven Stover/DVIDS
32: © Senior Chief Petty Officer Jayme Pastoric/US Navy/DVIDS
34: © Petty Officer 2nd Class Shauntae Hinkle-Lymas/US Navy/DVIDS
37: © Petty Officer 1st Class Anthony Walker/US Navy/DVIDS
39: © Brad Houshour/US Navy/DVIDS
42: © Petty Officer 2nd Class Erika Manzano/US Navy/DVIDS
45: © Bill Stafford/NASA
47: © US Navy/DVIDS
50: © Pete Souza/White House
53: © Sgt. Marco Mancha/US Marine Corps/DVIDS
55: © Sgt. Daniel P. Shook/DVIDS
56: © Red Line Editorial

ABOUT THE AUTHOR

Tammy Gagne is an author and editor who specializes in nonfiction. She has written hundreds of books for both children and adults. She lives in northern New England with her husband, son, and dogs.